First Facts®

Animal Rulers

KINGS OF THE RIVERS

Jody S. Rake

raintree

a Capstone company — publishers for children

Raintree is an imprint of Capstone Global Library Limited, a company incorporated in England and Wales having its registered office at 264 Banbury Road, Oxford, OX2 7DY – Registered company number: 6695582

www.raintree.co.uk
myorders@raintree.co.uk

Edited by Adrian Vigliano
Designed by Kayla Rossow
Picture research by Kelly Garvin
Production by Kathy McColley
Originated by Captsone Global Library Limited
Printed and bound in the United Kingdom.

ISBN 978 1 4747 4865 0 (hardback)
21 20 19 18 17
10 9 8 7 6 5 4 3 2 1

ISBN 978 1 4747 4871 1 (paperback)
22 21 20 19 18
10 9 8 7 6 5 4 3 2 1

British Library Cataloguing in Publication Data
A full catalogue record for this book is available from the British Library.

Acknowledgements
We would like to thank the following for permission to reproduce photographs: Alamy/Bill Bachman, 17; Minden Pictures: Flip Nicklin, 13, Franco Banfi/NPL, 15; Newscom/Paulo de Oliveira/NHPA/Photoshot, 21; Shutterstock: Dmitry Naumov, cover (middle), Emi, 9, eye-blink, 5, Foto593, cover (top middle), Kletr, cover (top right), 19, mamahoohooba, cover (bottom), Michal Ninger, cover (top left), ostill, 11, Utopia_88, 7; artistic elements: Shutterstock: ananas, basel101658, DeshaCAM, Dmitry Naumov, Jeane09, legin37, mamahoohooba, Nebojsa Kontic, sabri deniz kizil, sebos, shulgenko, skelos, Vladimir Wrangel

We would like to thank Jackie Gai for her invaluable help in the preparation of this book.

Contents

Go with the flow

All around Earth you can find rivers that are full of life. Rivers are always in motion.

River water is fresh, not salty. Rivers contain **food chains**. There are **predators** in these food chains. They are the rulers of their watery world!

predator animal that hunts other animals for food

food chain series of plants and animals in which each one in the series eats the one before it

Fact! The longest river in the world is the Nile River in Africa. It stretches 6,853 kilometres (4,258 miles) from central Africa to the Mediterranean Sea.

Alligators and crocodiles

Alligators and crocodiles live in warm rivers all over the world. These speedy **reptiles** swim up to 32 kilometres (20 miles) per hour. Their strong eyesight and sense of smell help make them top predators. They will eat anything they can catch, including fish, turtles, birds, pigs and even buffalo.

reptile cold-blooded animal that breathes air and has a backbone; most reptiles have scales

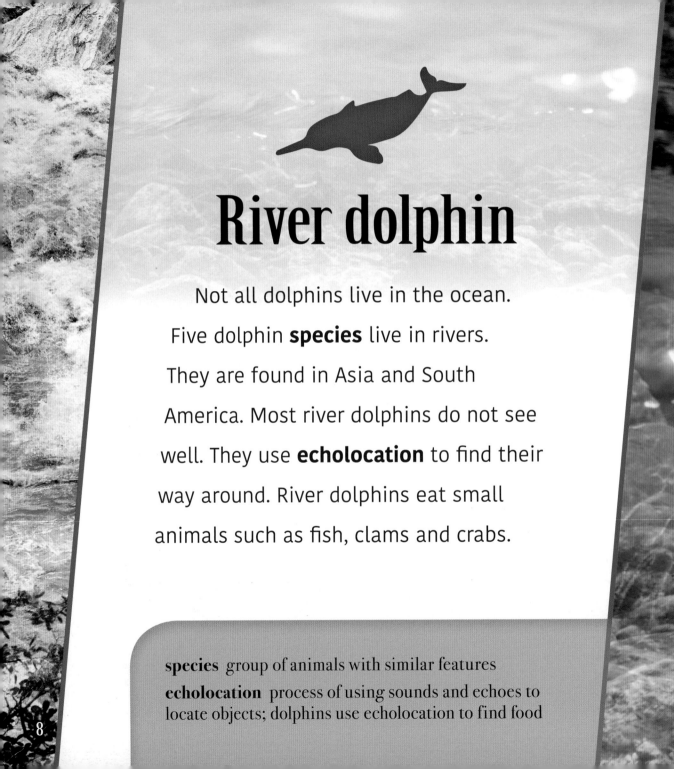

River dolphin

Not all dolphins live in the ocean. Five dolphin **species** live in rivers. They are found in Asia and South America. Most river dolphins do not see well. They use **echolocation** to find their way around. River dolphins eat small animals such as fish, clams and crabs.

species group of animals with similar features

echolocation process of using sounds and echoes to locate objects; dolphins use echolocation to find food

River otter

River otters' **flexible** bodies make them strong swimmers. Their smooth waterproof fur helps them glide through water. River otters live in all **continents** except Australia and Antarctica. Their diet includes fish, frogs and snakes.

The 1.5-metre (5-foot) giant otter is the largest of all river otters. It is one of the top predators of the river Amazon.

flexible able to bend or move easily
continent one of Earth's seven large land masses

Fact! River otters are related to weasels and skunks.

11

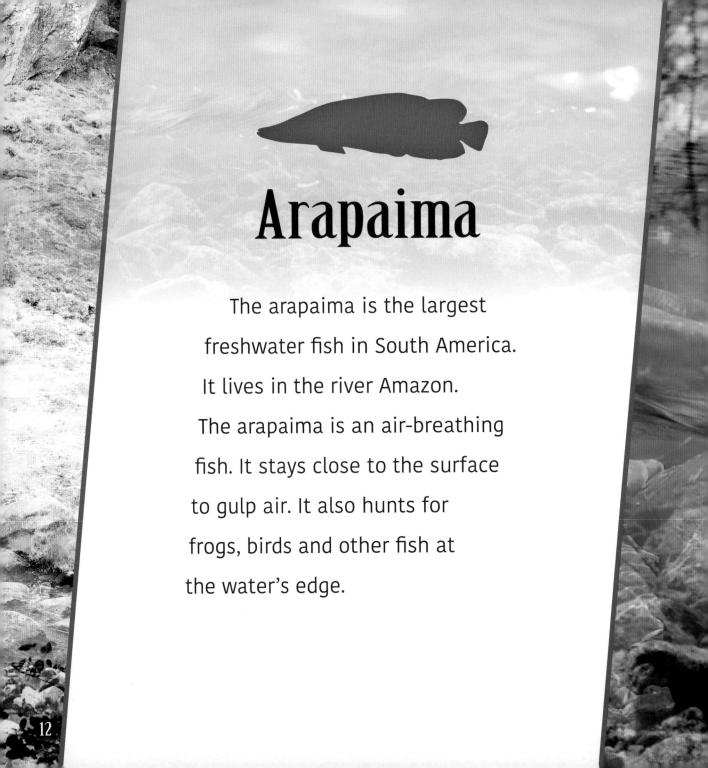

Arapaima

The arapaima is the largest freshwater fish in South America. It lives in the river Amazon. The arapaima is an air-breathing fish. It stays close to the surface to gulp air. It also hunts for frogs, birds and other fish at the water's edge.

Giant freshwater stingray

The giant freshwater stingray lives in the rivers of Asia. This fish can grow to 5 metres (16.5 feet) long. Its long tail has a 38-centimetre (15-inch) stinger. The stinger has a powerful **toxin**. Stingrays use their stingers for **defence**, not for hunting. The stingray stays mainly at the bottom and hunts for clams and crabs.

toxin poison

defence way to protect someone or something from an attack

Fact! The giant freshwater stingray wasn't discovered until 1990.

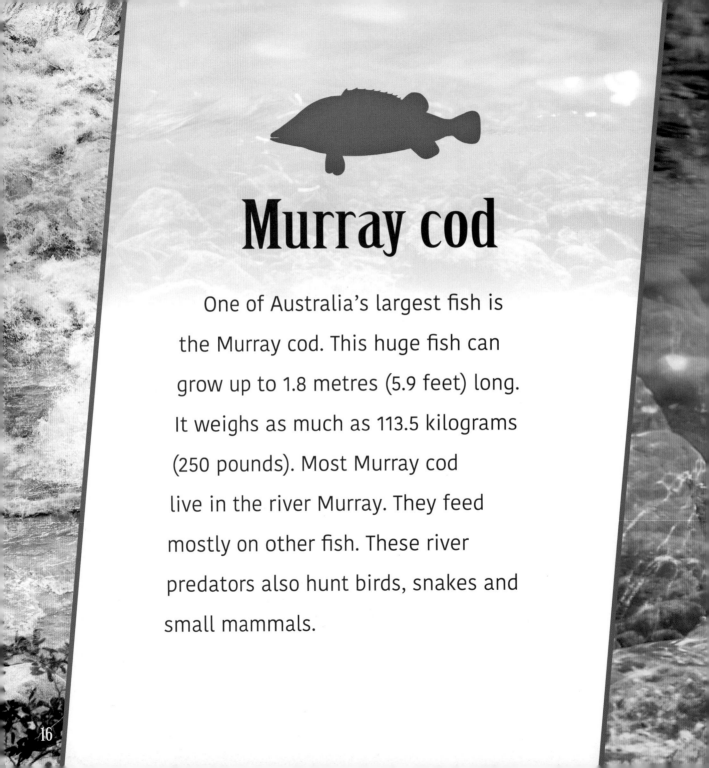

Murray cod

One of Australia's largest fish is the Murray cod. This huge fish can grow up to 1.8 metres (5.9 feet) long. It weighs as much as 113.5 kilograms (250 pounds). Most Murray cod live in the river Murray. They feed mostly on other fish. These river predators also hunt birds, snakes and small mammals.

Catfish

Catfish live in rivers all over the world. Most catfish eat plants and small animals. The Mekong giant catfish of Asia can be up to 3 metres (10 feet) long and weigh 295 kilograms (650 pounds). That's bigger than a tiger! Unlike a tiger, the Mekong catfish eats mostly plants.

prey animal hunted by another animal for food

Fact! The electric catfish of northern Africa uses electricity to stun its **prey**.

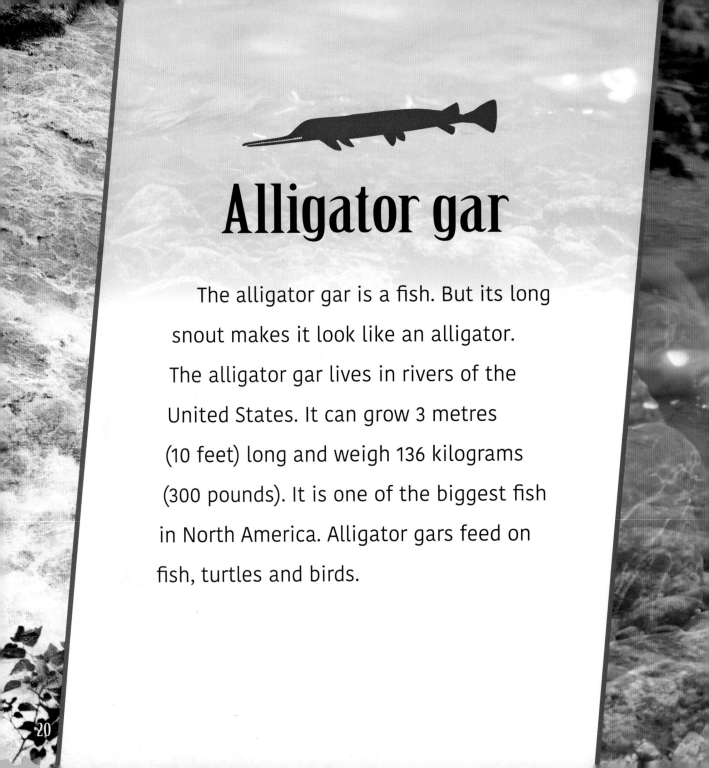

Alligator gar

The alligator gar is a fish. But its long snout makes it look like an alligator. The alligator gar lives in rivers of the United States. It can grow 3 metres (10 feet) long and weigh 136 kilograms (300 pounds). It is one of the biggest fish in North America. Alligator gars feed on fish, turtles and birds.

Glossary

continent one of Earth's seven large land masses

defence way to protect someone or something from an attack

echolocation process of using sounds and echoes to locate objects; dolphins use echolocation to find food

flexible able to bend or move easily

food chain series of plants and animals in which each one in the series eats the one before it

predator animal that hunts other animals for food

prey animal hunted by another animal for food

reptile cold-blooded animal that breathes air and has a backbone; most reptiles have scales

species group of animals with similar features

toxin poison

Find out more

Books

River (Life Cycles), Sean Callery (Kingfisher, 2013)

River Food Chains (Food Chains and Webs), Angela Royston (Heinemann Library, 2015)

Rivers (Geography Corner), Ruth Thomson (Wayland, 2013)

Websites

www.dkfindout.com/uk/animals-and-nature/fish/rays
Learn all about rays on this website.

gowild.wwf.org.uk/regions/americas-fact-files/river-dolphin
Find out more about river dolphins and listen to the sounds they make.

Comprehension questions

1. List two things about rivers and how you think they are different from oceans.

2. Study the picture of the river dolphin on page 9. Then study the picture of the otter on page 11. What similarities do these animals have? How are they different?

3. River dolphins have poor eyesight, so they use echolocation to find their way around. What is echolocation? Hint: Use the glossary for help!

Index